Story & Art by
Mika
Yamamori

CONTENTS

STORY THUS FAR

Suzume Yosano is a second-year in high school. Born in the country, she grew up living a free and easy life. Due to family circumstances, she was forced to transfer to a school in Tokyo. Lost on her first day in the city, she is found by a man who later turns out to be her homeroom teacher, Mr. Shishio. Suzume gradually develops feelings for him.

When Shishio breaks up with her, Suzume is devastated, but with the help of her friends, she finds the strength to move forward.

Suzume and friends enter their second year of high school, but there's a problem. The first-year girls just can't get enough of Mamura and pester him to no end, so Mamura's friends come up with a plan to turn Suzume into his fake girlfriend to run them off. On their final day as a fake couple, Mamura takes Suzume to the aquarium—the same one she visited with Shishio! Just as Suzume is overcome by her memories of Shishio, Mamura suddenly declares his love to her.

Suzume spends the night weighing her time with Shishio against her feelings for Mamura and finally comes to a decision...

Daytime Shooting Star
Day 61

DAYTIME SHOOTING STAR

SIZZ
SIZZLE
HUP.

YUP, LOOKS GOOD.
SIZZLE
SIZZLE
FRENCH TOAST IS HARDER TO MAKE THAN I THOUGHT.
I HOPE DAICHI LIKES IT.
He's been asking for French toast.
DING-DONG
SIZZLE
IT'S A BIT EARLY FOR VISITORS. I WONDER WHO IT IS...
JUST WHEN I FINALLY GOT THE HANG OF IT TOO.
OH. JUST A MINUTE.
TAP
TAP
TAP
TAP
YES?
CLICK
PANIC
OH, DAIKI'S UP.
What a relief.
PHEW

HAA
HAA
HAA
...

WHA...
WHAT ARE YOU...
...DOING?
MY ANSWER...
I CAME TO GIVE YOU MY ANSWER.

NOW...?
YES, NOW!
SCRITCH
SCRITCH
OKAY...
GO AHEAD.
I'M LISTENING.
...

I...
I'M GOING TO BE HONEST WITH YOU.
WHEN I'M WITH MR. SHISHIO...
...IT'S NOTHING LIKE BEING WITH YOU...
WHEN HE AND I ARE TOGETHER...
...ALL I WANT TO DO IS BE NEAR HIM.
BUT EVEN WHEN I AM, I STILL FEEL ANXIOUS AND UNCERTAIN.
AND AS HAPPY AS HE MAKES ME, I CAN'T HELP BUT FEEL INSECURE. IT'S PAINFUL.

BUT YOU...
YOU'RE ALWAYS RIGHT THERE...
NO MATTER WHAT, I CAN ALWAYS COUNT ON YOU.
I DON'T SECOND-GUESS MYSELF OR WHAT I SAY AROUND YOU EITHER.
WIGGLE
WHEN WE'RE TOGETHER, I FEEL CALM.
YOU'VE CHEERED ME UP SO MANY TIMES JUST BY BEING BY MY SIDE.
BUT...

...IF YOU ASK ME IF THIS IS LOVE...
...HONESTLY, I DON'T KNOW!
I'M SORRY...
I SEE...
WELL...

...THAT'S HOW I FELT UNTIL LAST NIGHT.

AND THIS IS HOW I FEEL NOW.

HUH...?

I've still got more to say.

BUT WHEN I REALLY THINK ABOUT IT...

IT FEELS WRONG TO COMPARE HOW I FEEL WITH MR. SHISHIO TO HOW I FEEL WITH YOU.

YOU'RE TWO COMPLETELY DIFFERENT PEOPLE. IT WOULD BE WEIRD IF I FELT THE SAME WAY ABOUT BOTH OF YOU.

BESIDES...

...IF I WERE TO TURN YOU DOWN NOW...
...NOTHING WOULD CHANGE...
MY FEELINGS FOR MR. SHISHIO WOULD CONTINUE TO WEIGH ME DOWN.
...I'M STILL WORKING OUT MY FEELINGS.
SO, I UNDERSTAND IF THIS SOUNDS CONDE-SCENDING, BUT...
OF COURSE...
THERE'S EVEN A CHANCE I MAY BE USING YOU.

I PROMISE I'LL DO MY BEST TO ONLY THINK OF YOU.
SO...
...IF...
...YOU'RE OKAY WITH THAT...
...AND DON'T MIND KILLING TIME WITH ME...
...OR VOLUNTEERING TO HELP ME OUT, THEN...
BDMP
BDMP
I...
BDMP

I'D LIKE TO BE YOUR GIRLFRIEND.

BLUSH
I...
...DID IT!!
THAT...
B...BUT I PUT A LOT OF THOUGHT INTO IT.
I KNOW.
...DIDN'T MAKE ANY SENSE AT ALL!
?!
?!
FLICK
I KNOW YOU DID, IDIOT.

I PROMISE...
...I'LL TAKE EVEN BETTER CARE OF YOU THAN BEFORE.
I HOPE YOU'LL DO THE SAME.

...
THANK YOU...
...
BLUSH
...
...
...
BLUSH
KLACK
DAIKI?
WHAT'S TAKING SO LONG? IS IT THE NEWSPAPER SALESMAN AGAIN?
OH?
MISS YOSANO?
OH! GOOD MORNING!
...

I DIDN'T EXPECT TO FIND YOU HERE SO EARLY.
OH... I WAS JUST DELIVERING A MESSAGE... WELL! I'D BETTER HEAD BACK HOME. I HAVEN'T HAD BREAKFAST YET.
WELL, WHY DON'T YOU STAY FOR–
I'M FINE!!
WELL... GOODBYE!
HUT
HEY!
SEE YOU AT SCHOOL.
UH...
UH-HUH!

THERE'S PLENTY OF FRENCH TOAST TO GO AROUND.
MORN-ING...
OH, GOOD MORNING, DAICHI.
OH!
YAWN
YAY!! FRENCH TOAST!!
CAN I EAT DAIKI'S?
JUST A SECOND, DAICHI. I'LL MAKE YOU SOME RIGHT NOW.
ARE YOU SURE SHE COULDN'T JOIN US?
HERE.
TAKE IT.
SCRAPE

I'M NOT HUNGRY.
HAA
HAA
HAA
HAA

HAA
HAA
"WOULD YOU BE MY FRIEND?"
MAYBE...
MAYBE WHAT I'M DOING IS WRONG.

...IS...

...IT...?

"I THINK THERE'S SOMEONE MUCH BETTER OUT THERE WAITING FOR HIM."

UNTIL RECENTLY, I REALLY BELIEVED THAT.

HE'S SUCH A GOOD FRIEND. I JUST WANTED HIM TO BE HAPPY.

I NEVER THOUGHT I'D BE THE ONE CAST IN THAT ROLE.

"I HOPE YOU'LL DO THE SAME."
GU...

I NEVER THOUGHT I'D EVER BE ABLE...
...TO MAKE SOMEONE HAPPY.
UU...
...GUH...
SOB.

ARE THESE...
...TEARS OF JOY...
...OR SOMETHING ELSE?
AT THIS POINT...

...IT'S HARD TO SAY, BUT...

...I KNOW ONE THING FOR SURE....

...THIS IS THE BEGINNING OF MY SECOND LOVE.

And so...

We've reached volume 10...!!
I never once imagined this series would run this long...! Thank you all very much for your support!

The story has taken many twists and turns, but as anxiety-inducing as the plot can be, it pales in comparison to my deadlines!!
I was buried. I thought I'd never see the light of day again!!

Anyway, enough about that...

I hope you enjoy *Daytime Shooting Star* volume 10!

YUCK
I cut my hair and it ended up looking like my mom's.
She said my bedhead looked terrible.

DAYTIME SHOOTING STAR
Day 62

DAYTIME SHOOTING STAR

SCREE
BUT I WON'T...
... ...
...
...
I'M YOURS...
I'D LIKE TO BE YOUR GIRLFRIEND.
...
MAAAMUU...

...RA!
SLAP!
A-ARE YOU OKAY?! I DIDN'T MEAN TO HIT YOU SO HARD...
OW...
MUTTER
BONK
SLIP
?!
GUESS THAT MEANS...
...IT WASN'T A DREAM.
FOR THE FIRST TIME IN MY LIFE...
...I HAVE A BOYFRIEND.
WHAT'S THIS?

SUZUME? SPORTING A BUN? TALK ABOUT UNUSUAL!
You're right.
I WENT FOR A RUN THIS MORNING AND WAS WORRIED MY HAIR MIGHT SMELL.
WHAT?! YOU DIDN'T TAKE A SHOWER?!
I DIDN'T HAVE TIME.
THAT'S DISGUST-ING!!
But I did wipe myself down.
Wiped yourself down...?!
OH.
It's Suzume and the others.

M...
MORNING...!
There she goes, clenching that strap again.
HUH? WHAT'S WRONG, SUZUME?
YOU LOOK A LITTLE FLUSH...
...
YO...

What?
...
SOMETHING STRANGE IS GOING ON.
...
...
What...??
What??
Huh...??
ARE...

...YOU SERIOUS?!
NOD
UH...
UH-HUH...
Ugh... You shouldn't stuff your face like that.
OMIGOSH! I'M SO HAPPY FOR YOU! I FEEL LIKE MY HEART MIGHT BURST FROM EXCITEMENT!!
OKAY, SPILL! WHO BROUGHT IT UP FIRST? YOU OR MAMURA?!
I GUESS THAT... MAYBE... WE BOTH DID...?
WHAT?! WHAT DO YOU MEAN? THAT SOUNDS DEEP...!!
WOW... SUZUME AND MAMURA... WHO WOULD'VE THOUGHT...?
I see, I see...
KAME'S MIC
Have some bell pepper.
BUT...
DOESN'T IT FEEL GREAT?
YOU'VE FOUND...
...YOUR NEXT LOVE.

We should throw a party.

You just want an excuse to have fun, Kame.

Then it's your treat.

Huh?

MY "NEXT...

...LOVE"...

Bye!

See ya.

WHERE ARE THE OTHERS?

HUH?

TSURU'S WITH INUKAI, KAME HAD TO WORK AND YUYUKA HAS A MEETING...
HMM...
THEN...
I'LL WALK YOU PARTWAY HOME.
UM...
OKAY...
BUT...
...IT'S A LITTLE TOO SOON...
...TO CALL IT THAT.

WE'VE WALKED HOME TOGETHER BEFORE...
...BUT I FEEL EVEN MORE TENSE THAN USUAL.
LITTLE BY LITTLE...
MAMURA...
...AND I...
TAKE IT ONE STEP AT A TIME.
Faculty Room

TLE
EXCUSE ME.
I'M FROM THE BEAU-TIFICATION COMMITTEE...
RAT
HUH?
OH...
WELL, IF IT ISN'T NEKOTA!
It's been a while.
UGH.
GUT REACTION
UGH?
AND WHAT'S WITH THAT FACE, NEKOTA?
Humph.
OKAY. SO DID YOU NEED HELP OR...?
I'M ON THE BEAUTIFICATION COMMITTEE, BUT THE STORAGE LOCKER IN THE BACK IS BROKEN...
YOU'RE KIDDING...
When is it not broken?

WELL...SHALL WE GO HAVE A LOOK?
HUH?!
WITH YOU?!
DO YOU SEE ANYONE ELSE HERE?
Shall we go then?
THIS GUY...
AFTER EVERYTHING THAT'S HAPPENED... HE'S GOT SOME NERVE!!
GRR
I hope you go bald.
I KNOW WHAT YOU DID!!
HOW DARE YOU TOY WITH A YOUNG GIRL'S HEART!!
YOU SAID THE STORAGE LOCKER, RIGHT?
THE SOCCER TEAM IS OFTEN OVER THERE...
MR. SHISHIO?
HUH?
OH, SORRY.

LET'S GO.
HMM...
DID YOU HEAR? MAMURA AND SUZUME ARE DATING NOW.
ISN'T THAT AMAZING?
YEAH...
I HEAR IT'S ALL AN ACT TO THROW EVERYONE OFF.
LOOKS LIKE THEY'RE STILL AT IT.
OH, YOU MEAN YOU DON'T KNOW?

THOSE TWO ARE DATING FOR REAL NOW.
TAKE THAT.
HE'LL PROBABLY JUST LAUGH IT OFF LIKE ALWAYS...

ARE YOU...
...SERIOUS?
UH...
MR. SHISHIO?
SORRY!
WHAP
IT JUST...
...CAUGHT ME BY SURPRISE...
ERM...

YES, THAT'S RIGHT...THE STORAGE!

...

COULD IT BE...

...THAT MR. SHISHIO...

...
...
UH...
UM...
WELL...

BDMP

HUH?
MAMURA?
WHAT'S WRONG?
DO YOU NEED TO TELL ME SOMETHING?
IS IT ABOUT THE HOME-WORK?
...
MAMURA?

DON'T YOU...
...WANT TO...
...STAY A LITTLE LONGER?
WHAT?!
M-MAMURA... I DIDN'T KNOW YOU WERE THAT KIND OF GUY!
I'M NOT...
...BUT IF I STAYED QUIET, YOU WOULDN'T HAVE NOTICED!

WHAT I MEAN IS...
DON'T MAKE ME HAVE TO SPELL IT OUT, DUMMY.
CAN'T YOU READ BETWEEN THE LINES, IDIOT?

I'M...
...SORRY...
...
...
...
...
I'M GOING HOME...
WHAT?
BUT YOU JUST...
IT'S NOT SAFE FOR YOU TO BE OUT TOO LATE.
SO LONG.
UM...
MAMURA...

SEE YOU TOMORROW...
...AT SCHOOL.
YEAH.

THAT GOODBYE...
...WAS A LITTLE DIFFERENT THAN YESTERDAY'S.

THERE'S STILL TOO MUCH DISTANCE BETWEEN US TO CALL THIS LOVE...

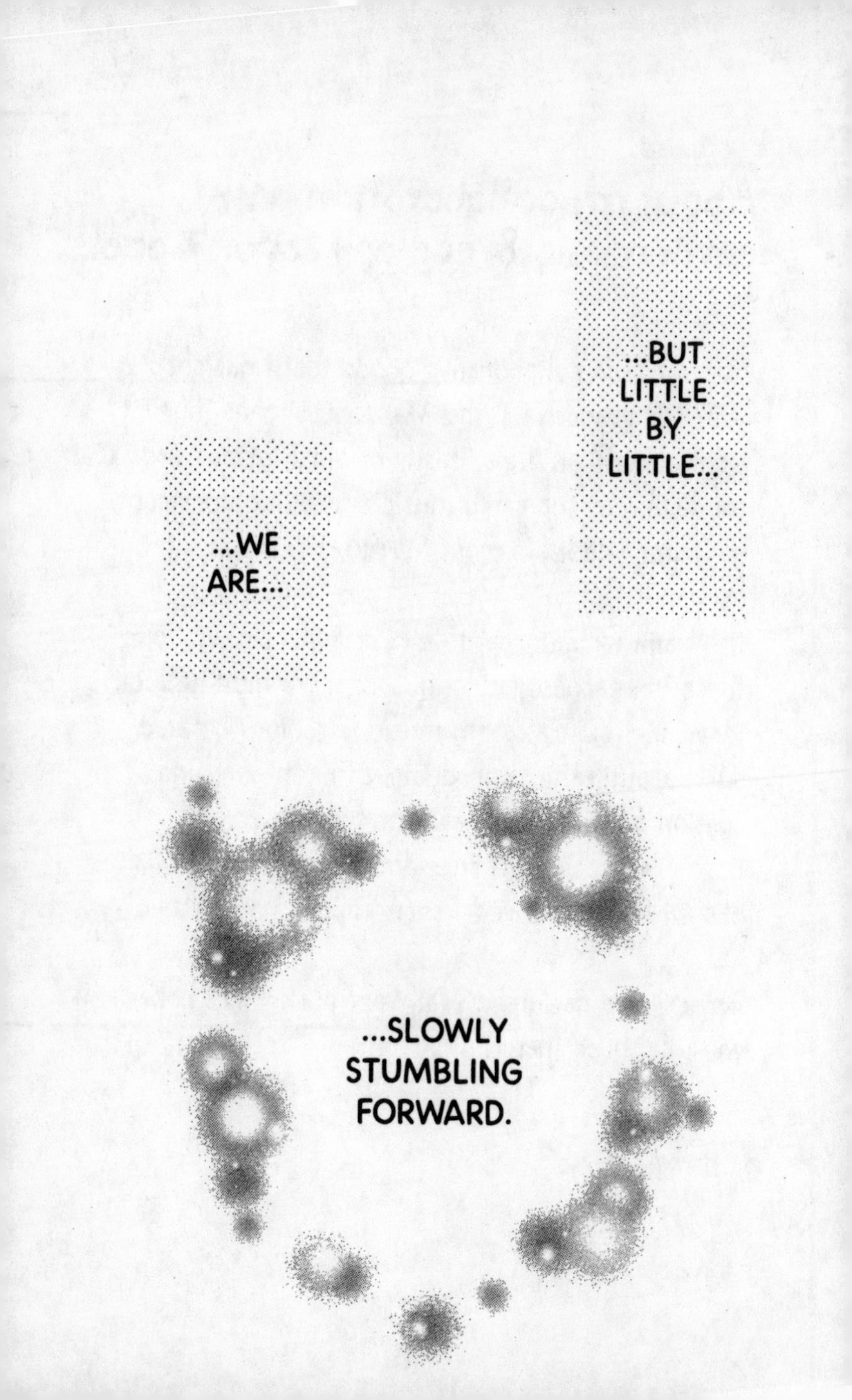

...BUT
LITTLE
BY
LITTLE...

...WE
ARE...

...SLOWLY
STUMBLING
FORWARD.

About my collaboration with earth music & ecology Japan Label...

The *Daytime* collaborative goods that I designed with our readers for the *Margaret* Dream Tour went on sale on June 7! Our original images were on display at the earth music & ecology storefront in Shimo-Kitazawa from May 10-18! Thank you all very much.
It all still feels unreal to me. For this Dream Tour, three high school students sent me a multitude of ideas. The staff at earth music & ecology created such beautiful final products. After the briefing session, all I did was get drunk at dinner and do my impression of Brandon from *Beverly Hills 90210*! I'm very sorry! I even impersonated David!

Anyway, the designs are all very pretty, so I hope you will check them out!

DAYTIME SHOOTING STAR
Day 63

DATING...

...IS STRANGE.

"DON'T YOU..."

"...WANT TO STAY A LITTLE LONGER?"

DAYTIME SHOOTING STAR

I NEVER THOUGHT I'D HEAR...
...HIM SAY SOMETHING LIKE THAT...
"MY BOY-FRIEND"...
I GUESS THAT'S WHAT HE IS...
WHAT'S WRONG? DOES IT TASTE BAD?
WHAT?!
NO. IT'S REALLY GOOD!
HUH?
I HOPE YOU'RE NOT LYING.
YOU KNOW, YOU SEEM A LITTLE DISTRACTED LATELY.
YEAH, I'VE GOT SOME STUFF GOING ON WITH MAMURA...
MAMURA?!

YOU MEAN THAT NICE-LOOKING BOY?
YEAH.
WE STARTED DATING RECENTLY...
...BUT I DON'T KNOW MUCH ABOUT RELATIONSHIPS.
STARTLED
WHAT?!
YOU'RE DATING... REALLY?!
OH NO!!
UH... UNCLE...
I NEED TO LEARN WHEN TO KEEP MY MOUTH SHUT.
OH...? IS THAT SO? HMM...
WELL, I GUESS YOU'RE AT THAT AGE...
...BUT SINCE WHEN?!
DON'T LEAVE OUT A SINGLE DETAIL... HA HA HA HA!
UH...
OH, YES...

YOU SHOULD INVITE HIM OVER THIS SUNDAY.
OKAY?!
...
MATRYOSHKA-TIZED
21:29
From Suzume Yosano
Do you happen to have plans this Sunday?
BZZZ
BZZZ
BZZZ
Not really.
WHY SO POLITE ...?
RUSTLE
RUSTLE
BZZZ
BZZZ

21:29
From Suzume Yosano
Why don't you come by for a visit this Sunday?
21:30
From Suzume Yosano
Uncle insists I bring you by... I'm scared.
...
♪ RING-A-LING ♫
Got it. I'll be there at 1:00 p.m.
WHEW.
I DID IT.
COME TO THINK OF IT...
...THIS WILL BE MAMURA'S FIRST TIME HERE.

...
I WONDER WHAT GIRLS USUALLY DO...
...WHEN THEIR BOYFRIEND COMES OVER.
MAMURA'S GOING TO VISIT YOU?
YES, BUT I DON'T KNOW WHAT WE SHOULD DO.
THE ONLY GAME MY UNCLE HAS IS *LIFE*.
I WONDER WHY HE HAS THAT GAME...
WHY DON'T YOU LEAF THROUGH OLD YEAR-BOOKS TOGETHER?
WHEN YOU'RE DONE, YOU CAN WATCH DVDS.
I SEE.
What about *Uno*?
Uno... Hmm... Not sure about that.
"ARE YOU..."

"...SERIOUS?"
ON THE OFF CHANCE...
...MR. SHISHIO STILL LIKES THAT BUMPKIN...
IF SHE WERE...
...TO SOMEHOW...
...FIND OUT ABOUT IT, THEN...
...

MAYBE...

...SOMETHING WILL HAPPEN.

HUH?

SOME-THING?

HMPH... YOU KNOOOW.

MAYBE SOME HUGGING OR KISSING ACTION.

WIGGLE

WIGGLE

EWW!

BOOOOOOO!!

N-NO... NO WAY!!

HUH? WHY NOT? ISN'T THAT WHAT COUPLES DO?

B-BUT WE HAVEN'T BEEN DATING THAT LONG.

THAT DOESN'T MATTER.

YU... YUYUKA...!

NOT INTERESTED.

TSURU, YOU AGREE THAT IT'S TOO EARLY, RIGHT?!

UH...

UM...

YES, WELL...

Huh...?

Hmm... So, they've at least kissed.

ANYWAY...

YOU SHOULD BE PREPARED JUST IN CASE.

WE'LL BE EXPECTING A FULL REPORT ON MONDAY!
...
SH...
SHE DIDN'T HAVE TO PUT ME...
...ON THE SPOT BACK THERE.
HOW DO I EVEN PREPARE FOR SOME-THING LIKE THAT?
I DON'T EVEN KNOW WHERE TO BEGIN.
...
A KISS...

I DID GET PRETTY CLOSE ONCE.
OH!
THUMP THUMP THUMP THUMP
NO, NO... UNCLE WILL BE THERE ANYWAY.
THE MOOD WON'T BE RIGHT.
YES!!
BUT...
...WHAT IF...
...

...THINGS DO HAPPEN TO HEAD IN THAT DIRECTION?

WHA...

...WHAT SHOULD I DO...?

IT WOULD BE WEIRD TO PUSH HIM AWAY. HE'S MY BOYFRIEND, AFTER ALL.

BUT...

...IS THAT WHAT I WANT?

MAYBE I SHOULDN'T LET IT GET TO THAT POINT.

IS IT NORMAL TO FEEL THIS WAY...?

Hmm...

Hmm...

...be clear about what I want.

But I really should...

Hmm... Hmm...

Hmm...

Hmm...

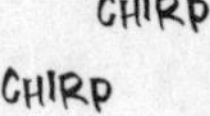

...
WHEW...
DING
DONG
CLACK
WELCOME.
HELLO...

UM... HERE...
MY DAD TOLD ME TO BRING THIS.
HUH?
OH, NOW... YOU DIDN'T HAVE TO DO...
KAMEJU'S DORAYAKI FROM ASAKUSA
Asakusa Kameju's Dorayaki
Kameju's Dorayaki
KA-KAMEJU'S DORAYAKI ...!!
This boy...is good!!
CLICK
W...
WELCOME...
YO...
A KATSURA SANSHI SCHTICK?

HOW ABOUT SOME TEA? I'LL CALL YOU WHEN IT'S READY.

OH, MAKE SURE YOU KEEP THIS DOOR OPEN.

...

...

YOU CAN SIT DOWN IF YOU WANT...
'KAY...
AFTER...
...WHAT EVERYONE SAID...
...I'M SUPER NER-VOUS...!!
GRIP
I KNOW! I'LL JUST TAKE TSURU'S ADVICE...
Look through some year-books...
...or watch DVDs.
VOICE FROM HEAVEN
HEY!

HOW ABOUT WE LOOK THROUGH SOME ALBUMS?!

Club Members Hot Springs

New Year's Party

...

WHAT'S WITH ALL THESE PICTURES OF YOUR UNCLE?

THIS IS ALL I COULD FIND...

TOOK OFF HIS JACKET

EPIC FAIL!

I FORGOT!! MY YEAR-BOOKS ARE ALL BACK AT HOME!!

THERE'S NO WAY HE'S ENJOYING THIS.

Where's the fun in looking at Uncle's old pictures?

IS THIS...

...YOU?
OH.
YOU'RE RIGHT...
I DIDN'T THINK THERE'D BE A PICTURE OF ME IN HERE.
THAT DOLL...
I HAD ONE JUST LIKE IT.
WHAT?!
HE WAS THE VILLAIN ON THAT ONE TV SHOW, RIGHT?
THAT'S RIGHT!! I LOVED THAT VILLAIN—EVEN MORE THAN THE HERO.
I KNOW WHAT YOU MEAN.
REALLY?!

I ALWAYS COPIED THE FUNNY WAY HE SPOKE.
HA HA...
I DID THAT TOO.
OH.
THAT'S THE THIRD TIME...
...HE'S LAUGHED.
EACH TIME HE LAUGHS...
...I FEEL A LITTLE MORE AT EASE.

I CAN'T IMAGINE MAMURA TALKING LIKE THAT VILLAIN.
BUT WHY ARE YOU POUTING IN ALL YOUR PICTURES?
HUH?
THERE'S NO WAY I AM.
FLIP
FLIP
JUST A SECOND. THERE HAS TO BE AT LEAST ONE...
...PICTURE OF ME SMILING...

WHAP
WHAT'D YOU DO THAT FOR?
UH... THAT'S ENOUGH OF THE PICTURES!!
WHAT ARE YOU TALKING ABOUT?
YOU DON'T NEED TO HIDE YOUR EMBARRASSING PICTURES FROM ME.
NO, THAT'S NOT IT...
THEN LET ME SEE THEM!
NUH-UH...
NO WAY...
NO...
...WAY!!
TUG

Memories
I SAID...
HUH...?

IS...
IS THIS...

...REALLY
HAPPENING...?

DAYTIME

Day 64

DAYTIME SHOOTING STAR

IS...
...THIS IT...?

WHA...

WHAT SHOULD I DO?!
BOMP
WHA...
HUH...?
WAIT...

UHHHHH!!
Memories
THUMP
Memories
WHAT KIND OF GUY DO YOU TAKE ME FOR?
DUMMY!
WHAT?
BLUUSH
IT...IT'S NOT W-W-WHAT YOU THINK!!
DON'T LIE!
It's not...?
SUZUME!
WILL YOU GIVE ME A HAND?

I'LL GO.
SST
OH... THANKS...
BY THE WAY...
I'M NOT GOING TO TRY ANYTHING, SO YOU CAN RELAX.

TUK
HUH...?
WHA...
WHAT IS THIS FEEL-ING...?
I WASN'T EXPECTING ANYTHING, SO...
...WHY DO I FEEL LIKE....
...HE REJECTED ME?
THERE MUST BE SOMETHING IN MY EYES.
RUB
RUB
...
BUT...

...I AM RELIEVED THAT IT ENDED BEFORE IT STARTED...
OH?
WHAT'S WRONG, MAMURA?
...
HEY, DID YOU HEAR ME?
WHOA!!
WOB
BLE

A-ARE YOU ALL RIGHT?
Do you have a fever?
I'M SORRY... I'M FINE...
IS THERE ANYTHING I CAN HELP WITH?
HUH? OH...
SHOULD I HAVE HIM HELP?
WELL, THINK YOU CAN POUR SOME TEA?
GLANCE
SO...
...THIS KID...
...IS SUZUME'S BOYFRIEND...

OH!
FIRST THINGS FIRST...!
AHEM
MA...
MAMURA, TELL ME WHAT YOU THINK OF SUZUME.
WHAT I THINK...?
I mean...
SUZUME IS MY ONE AND ONLY NIECE, YOU SEE. I CAN'T HELP BUT WORRY ABOUT HER.
SHE'S NOT THE MOST EXPERIENCED WHEN IT COMES TO DATING...
...AND SHE TENDS TO OVERTHINK THINGS.
TRUE...
AND...

THINGS DIDN'T END WELL...
...FOR HER WITH THE PREVIOUS GUY.
I NEVER WANT...
...TO SEE HER THAT HEARTBROKEN AGAIN.

KREE
WHAT'S TAKING MAMURA SO LONG?
GURGLE GURGLE
HUH?
OH?
THEY'RE HAVING A CONVERSATION...
I WONDER WHAT THEY'RE TALKING ABOUT.
HA HA HA HA!
SORRY ABOUT THAT.
I DIDN'T MEAN TO GET SO INTENSE.
UNFORTUNATELY, THE OLDER I GET, THE MORE I LECTURE PEOPLE.

I WANT YOU TO KNOW...
...THAT I'M TAKING YOUR QUESTION SERIOUSLY.
I'M NOT VERY GOOD...
...AT EXPRESSING MYSELF, BUT...
...I WILL DO MY BEST NOT TO MAKE HER CRY.

AND...
...I GET THAT YOU MIGHT BE CONCERNED ABOUT, WELL, YOU KNOW...
...BUT YOU DON'T NEED TO WORRY ABOUT ANYTHING LIKE THAT.
?!
WAIT... WHAT ARE THOSE TWO TALKING ABOUT...?!
HUH?? I DON'T KNOW WHAT YOU'RE GETTING AT!
That couldn't be further from my mind...
...
WELL... TO BE HONEST...
I'M A GUY, SO...
...STUFF HAPPENS, BUT...
BUT...

RIGHT NOW...
...I ONLY HOLD HALF HER HEART.
I THINK I CAN WAIT UNTIL SHE'S READY TO GIVE ME THE WHOLE THING.
IN ANY CASE...
I'M FINE WITH THE WAY THINGS ARE FOR NOW.

MAMURA...
KREE
TUK
I SEE...
I'M RELIEVED TO HEAR YOU SAY THAT.
Although that "for now" concerns me...
I DIDN'T REALIZE YOU CARE SO MUCH ABOUT HER.
I'D DO ANYTHING TO MAKE HER HAPPY...

...EVEN IF THAT MEANS WALKING AWAY.
I THINK...
...IN MY RUSH TO MOVE ON FROM MR. SHISHIO...
...I MISTAKENLY TRIED TO FORCE MAMURA AND MYSELF INTO THIS MOLD OF WHAT I BELIEVED A COUPLE SHOULD BE.
I TOLD HIM THAT I WOULD ONLY THINK OF HIM, BUT...

...I DID SO WITHOUT CONSIDERING MY OWN FEELINGS...

...OR MAMURA'S.

I...

I DON'T DESERVE SOMEONE AS KIND AS HIM.

I'M NOT WORTHY.

CLACK
HEY...
I BROUGHT US SOME DORAYAKI CAKES...
UH...
WHAT ARE YOU DOING?
OH, THIS?
I THOUGHT IT MIGHT BE FUN TO PLAY *THE GAME OF LIFE*.
THE GAME OF LIFE...?
COME HAVE A SEAT!! IT'S ALL SET UP!!

I MAY NOT LOOK IT, BUT I'M A MASTER AT THIS GAME!
IS THAT SO?
I SHOULD WARN YOU THAT THE ODDS OF ME WINDING UP AS A PROFESSIONAL BASEBALL PLAYER ARE PRETTY HIGH.
WHO CARES ...?

Isn't it better to be a doctor?
IT MAY STILL BE A WHILE...
...BEFORE MY FEELINGS CATCH UP TO MAMURA'S.

...WANT TO BECOME SOMEONE...

...WORTHY OF HIS AFFECTION.

ARE YOU SURE YOU DON'T WANT TO STAY FOR DINNER?

I DON'T WANT TO WEAR OUT MY WELCOME. MAYBE NEXT TIME.
REALLY? WHAT'S YOUR FAVORITE DISH? I'LL MAKE IT FOR YOUR NEXT VISIT.
GRATIN, I GUESS...
YOU GOT IT.
Thumbs up.
I'LL GO SEE MAMURA OFF...
ALL RIGHT. JUST BE CAREFUL.
THANKS SO MUCH...
...FOR COMING BY TODAY.
AND FOR THE DORAYAKI.
SURE.
...
MAMURA...

WHUSH
TRY HOLDING YOUR ARMS LIKE THIS.
HUH?
WHAT FOR...?
THUP

?!
BDMP
BDMP
BDMP
BDMP
BDMP
GRIP
WELL...

SHUPAH
...SEE YA LATER!!
Y-YOU KNOW...
...AT SCHOOL!!
VROOM
...

THAT GIRL...

...IS TRYING TO KILL ME...

THIS IS...

...THE BEST I CAN DO FOR NOW.

I WANT TO...
... BECOME WORTHY OF MAMURA'S AFFECTION.

DAYTIME SHOOTING STAR

DAYTIME
Day 65
SHOOTING STAR

I KNEW MAMURA WOULD SMELL LIKE SOAP.

DAYTIME SHOOTING STAR

OH, GOOD MORNING, KAME AND TSURU.
MOR-NIIING!
IT'S TOO EARLY TO BE THAT CHIPPER.
BY THE WAY, SUZUME...
HOW WAS YOUR WEEKEND??
ANYTHING TO REPORT?
HUH?
UH...
NOT MUCH, REALLY!
WE JUST PLAYED LIFE.
SO, YOU REALLY DID PLAY A BOARD GAME...
I FEEL A LITTLE SORRY FOR MAMURA.
THAT'S IT? TALK ABOUT A LETDOWN!
...
Guess it's harder to make progress than I thought.

I WONDER IF HUGGING HIM WAS GOING A LITTLE TOO FAR...?
NO, NO!!
SLAP
I TOLD MAMURA I'D FOCUS MY ATTENTION ON HIM, SO OF COURSE IT WASN'T!!
YUP!!
SUZUME, AREN'T YOU COMING?
HA HA HA
NOW THAT WE'RE IN OUR SECOND YEAR, MAMURA DOESN'T SIT NEXT TO ME ANYMORE.

IT'S A LITTLE LONELY.
OR SO I THOUGHT, BUT...
...MAYBE THIS IS BETTER SINCE IT MAKES THINGS LESS EMBARRASSING.
Besides, we chose our own seats.
RATTLE
TAKE YOUR SEATS!
WE'RE GOING TO START MAKING PREPARATIONS FOR SPORTS DAY.
HERE, PASS THESE OUT.
OH, IS IT THAT TIME ALREADY?
SPORTS DAY?
?

WE HAVE A SPORTS DAY?
OH, THAT'S RIGHT... YOU WEREN'T HERE FOR SPORTS DAY LAST YEAR, SUZUME.
WE HELD IT A LITTLE BIT EARLIER LAST YEAR.
UGH... THIS IS THE WORST...
SIGH
THE WHOLE SCHOOL PARTICIPATES, AND WE'RE DIVIDED INTO RED, BLUE AND YELLOW TEAMS.
I THINK WE'RE RED THIS YEAR.
I SEE.
MAYBE THERE'S A BREAD-EATING CONTEST...
YOU'VE GOT FOOD ON THE BRAIN, DON'T YOU?
LET'S SEE... THE EVENTS ARE LISTED ON THE HANDOUT YOU JUST RECEIVED. ONCE YOU'VE CIRCLED THE EVENT YOU WISH TO ENTER, TURN IT BACK IN TO ME.
ALSO...
...EACH CLASS WILL NEED TO SELECT ONE RUNNER FOR THE RELAY RACE. ANYONE INTERESTED?
YOU MAY VOLUNTEER YOURSELF OR ONE OF YOUR CLASSMATES.
OKAY!

THEN I VOLUNTEER MAMURA!
HUH?
DITTO.
YOU RAN LAST YEAR TOO.
WHAT?
How annoying...

YUP, MUCH FASTER THAN YOU'D THINK.
HE RAN THE RELAY LAST YEAR TOO.
SHOCKING, I KNOW. SINCE HE DOESN'T SEEM TO BE THE SPORTY TYPE.
REALLY ...?
I DIDN'T EXPECT HIM TO BE A RELAY RUNNER...
ALSO...
IT SEEMS THEY'RE LOOKING FOR VOLUNTEERS TO MAKE POM-POMS AND HEADBANDS AFTER SCHOOL.

IF YOU'RE INTERESTED, PLEASE GATHER IN ROOM 3-2.
OH...
POM-POMS AND HEAD-BANDS ...?
!
OH, I KNOW!
YOU CAN'T WALK HOME WITH ME TODAY?

NO. THERE'S SOMETHING I HAVE TO DO.
...
I'M REALLY SORRY!
SPORTS DAY...
NOT HAPPY
IF I MAKE MAMURA A HEADBAND...
...I WONDER IF HE'LL USE IT?
HEH HEH HEH.
HE COULD EVEN WEAR IT DURING THE RELAY RACE.
IMAGE
Reminiscent of last century.

3-2
I CAN'T BELIEVE I CAME UP WITH SUCH A GOOD IDEA.
OH...
I THINK THIS IS THE CLASS-ROOM.
CLAT
I DON'T KNOW ANY OF THEM...
There are first- and third-year students here too.
...
WALLFLOWER
MAYBE I SHOULD HAVE BROUGHT SOMEONE WITH ME.
RATTLE
!!
WHOOPS...

SORRY...

HEEEY!
YOU'RE LATE, MR. SHISHIO!!
WHAT TOOK YOU SO LONG?!
AH, SORRY ABOUT THAT!
MY MEETING RAN LATE.
WE'VE BEEN WAITING FOR THESE SUPPLIES...
NO WAY!

TO THINK THAT I'D RUN INTO HIM HERE...
HE HAS CLASS 3-2 THIS YEAR...
I SHOULD HAVE REALIZED THIS COULD HAPPEN.
WHAT DO I DO?
I SHOULD SAY SOMETHING TO HIM.
IF I IGNORE HIM, IT'LL JUST MAKE THINGS MORE AWKWARD.
BUT...
WHAT SHOULD I SAY...AND HOW?
HEY, YOSANO!

DON'T JUST STAND THERE. GRAB SOME SUPPLIES.
UH... YES, SIR...
EACH PERSON HAS TO MAKE FIVE HEADBANDS AND FOUR POM-POMS.
AH, BUT MAYBE YOU'RE TOO CLUMSY TO PULL IT OFF...
WHAT...?

I MAY NOT LOOK IT, BUT I'M A POM-POM-MAKING MACHINE.
ALL RIGHT...
THEN INSTEAD OF MOVING YOUR LIPS, LET'S SEE YOU MOVE YOUR HANDS.
MR. SHISHIO!
YES?
What's the matter?
GRABBED THEM.
I WONDER...
...HOW LONG IT'S BEEN SINCE WE...
...LAST TALKED LIKE THIS?

I'VE MISSED IT...

You do this, then tie it.

OH!

NO, NO. FORGET ABOUT THAT!!
I HAVE TO CONCENTRATE ON MAKING HEADBANDS!!
THIS WILL REQUIRE MY FULL ATTENTION!!

Hmm... I guess I'll make the pom-poms first.

I...
I DID IT!!
PANT
PANT
PANT
IT'S A LITTLE CROOKED, BUT YOU CAN STILL TELL IT'S A HORSE.
I DID A PRETTY GOOD JOB! I THINK...
I WONDER...

...IF MAMURA WILL WEAR IT.
I just can't get enough of the old idol imagery from the previous century.
GASP
HUH?!
NO ONE'S HERE!?
WHERE'D EVERYONE GO?
ARE YOU FINALLY DONE?
EVERYONE ELSE HAS GONE HOME.
Rigoletto
OH...
I CAN'T BELIEVE YOU DIDN'T NOTICE.

I SEE...
BUT I MUST ADMIT...
...I'M IMPRESSED YOU WERE ABLE TO FINISH THAT MANY POM-POMS.
RUSTLE
WELL...
RUSTLE
I THOUGHT IT WOULD BE BEST TO DO THE EASIEST JOB FIRST.
THOSE CAME OUT FINE, BUT YOU DIDN'T MEET YOUR HEADBAND QUOTA.
URGH...
STILL...
...YOU DID A REALLY GOOD JOB ON THOSE.
LOOKS LIKE YOU'VE DISCOVERED A NEW SKILL, TWEET-
OH...

SORRY.
THAT WAS...
...AGAINST THE RULES.
IT'S FINE.
That was close...
YOU CAN CALL ME WHATEVER YOU WANT.
IT DOESN'T MAKE A DIFFERENCE TO ME.

THUD
I SAID IT...
THUD
THAT WAS MY BEST BLUFF.
MY VOICE WAVERED AT THE END...
I BETTER LEAVE BEFORE HE REALIZES IT.
WELL...
...I SHOULD...

MR...
...SHISHIO...?

DAYTIME SHOOTING STAR

DAYTIME SHOOTING STAR
Day 66

DAYTIME SHOOTING STAR

OH, YOU'RE HOME, SUZUME.
TMP
HOW WAS SCHOOL?
TMP
TMP
I'VE GOT YOUR DINNER RIGHT HERE.
SLAM
Huh...?
Is she...
...entering a rebellious phase...?

...
...SHISHIO...
MR....
PLEASE LET GO OF ME!

MR....
...SHISHIO...
NO.
SIGH

SHOVE
THAT...
THAT WAS...
I DON'T KNOW WHAT TO SAY...
BANG
RATTLE
OH?

MR. SHISHIO, YOU'RE STILL HERE?
HUH?
IS SOMETHING WRONG?
...
NO.

IT'S NOTHING.

I DIDN'T...

...INTEND FOR THINGS TO PLAY OUT LIKE THAT.

I WAS 100 PERCENT IN THE WRONG.

I SHOWED A COMPLETE LACK OF RESOLVE.

JUST WHAT AM I TRYING TO DO?
IS THIS SEAT TAKEN?
NO.
GO RIGHT AHEAD...
TA-DAAAH!
AND IN WALKED HIS EX-GIRLFRIEND. ♪

TSU... BOMI...?!
WHAT ARE YOU DOING HERE?
Scoot over, will ya?
COME NOW... YOU LOOK LIKE YOU'VE SEEN A GHOST.
I HAPPENED TO GET A JOB HERE, SO I'M BACK. WELL, TEMPORARILY.
You haven't seen me since vol. 4.
YOU HAVEN'T CHANGED AT ALL.
HOW'VE YOU BEEN? WELL, I HOPE.
OH, I'LL HAVE A DRAFT.
Coming right up!
SAME AS ALWAYS.
WHAT A BLAND ANSWER...
OH, THAT REMINDS ME...
HOW ARE THINGS GOING WITH SUZUME?

THERE'S NOTHING...
...GOING ON.
YOU'RE KIDDING! NOTHING?!
What did I buy him those aquarium tickets for then?
MUTTER
MUTTER
YEAH, WELL...
...I'M JUST NO GOOD FOR HER...
...IN MORE WAYS THAN ONE.

SO...
YOU'VE FINALLY REALIZED THAT YOU'RE NO GOOD?
Or should I say lazy?
WHAT?
HOW CAN I PUT THIS? YOU TEND TO UNDERMINE YOUR ROMANTIC RELATIONSHIPS.
HMM... WHAT'S ANOTHER WAY TO PUT IT...?
STAB
STAB
YOU PRIORITIZE SHIELDING YOURSELF FROM PAIN AND FOCUS ALL YOUR ATTENTION ON PROTECTING YOUR PRIDE...
...AND ALL THE WHILE, YOU HANG ON TO YOUR TRAUMA SO YOU CAN PLAY THE PART OF THE TRAGIC HERO.

DEATH BLOW
YOU'RE SORT OF LIKE A KID RUNNING AROUND IN CIRCLES.
Oh, and by "kid," I don't mean your looks.
I... I HAVE NO WORDS...
I HOPE SHE DIDN'T COME BACK JUST TO TELL ME THIS...
BUT...
YOU KNOW, IT MIGHT BE A GOOD IDEA TO SWALLOW YOUR PRIDE FOR ONCE.
EXCUSE ME! ONE ORDER OF CHICKEN MEATBALLS, PLEASE.

WHEN...
...IS THE BEST TIME TO GIVE HIM THIS?
WHAT WAS THAT ALL ABOUT?

WHY DID MR. SHISHIO DO THAT?
WHAT WAS HE THINKING?
AND WHAT MADE ME...
...SAY "NO"?
Oh...
STOP IT!!
JUST STOP THINKING ABOUT IT ALREADY!!
HE PROBABLY JUST STUMBLED!!
YES. THAT'S GOT TO BE IT!
Happens all the time.
I CAN'T THINK...

...OF ANY OTHER REASON.
RATTLE
!

UH, WAIT!
HEY, LISTEN...
When'd she get so fast?!
WHOOSH BAM BAM BAM
WAIT! TWEETIE!!

I DIDN'T MEAN...
...TO CALL HER THAT.
OH.
...
LOOK, ABOUT WHAT...
...HAPPENED YESTERDAY...
I HAVE TO COME UP...
...WITH A REASON.

A REASON?

I CAN'T THINK OF ANY.

I DIDN'T PLAN FOR ANY OF THAT TO HAPPEN...

LIAR.

THE TRUTH IS...

...I REGRET EVERY-THING...

THAT I COULDN'T ASK HER TO GO TO THE AQUARIUM AGAIN.

THAT I WAS LATE ON CHRISTMAS DAY.

THAT WE COULDN'T CELEBRATE HER BIRTHDAY PROPERLY.

THAT I LET GO OF HER HAND AT THE SHRINE ON NEW YEAR'S.

I SHOULD'VE OPENED UP TO YOU.

I'M SORRY THAT I MADE YOU SHED SO MANY TEARS.

ACTUALLY, I'VE ALWAYS...

AFTER ALL...

...THAT'S HAPPENED...

...WHAT CAN I POSSIBLY SAY?

"YOU KNOW, IT MIGHT BE A GOOD IDEA TO SWALLOW YOUR PRIDE FOR ONCE."

I LOVE YOU.

Daytime Shooting Star Vol. 10/End

DAYTIME SHOOTING STAR

DAYTIME SHOOTING STAR
BONUS: Inukai's Story

IN MIDDLE SCHOOL, I WAS BOTH STUDENT BODY PRESI-DENT AND SOCCER TEAM CAPTAIN.
(I WAS A DEFENSIVE MIDFIELDER)

MY FAVORITE SPORT IS SOCCER.

MY FAVORITE SUBJECTS ARE HISTORY AND MATH.

INUKAI!!
Volleyball Team
MY WEAK AREAS ARE...
TWIRL
TWIRL

HUH?
WELL, I DON'T HAVE ANY.
PLEASE! PLEASE SHOW ME YOUR HOMEWORK!!
WILL YOU PLEASE LOOK OVER MY SPEECH FOR THE NATIONAL ENGLISH SPEECH CONTEST?
CAN YOU PLEASE SUB IN THE UPCOMING GAME? WE DON'T HAVE ENOUGH PLAYERS!!
Oh!

IF I PUT IN THE EFFORT, I CAN EXCEL AT ANY SUBJECT OR SPORT.
FOR MATH I? CHECK IN MY DESK.
IF YOU LIKE, I CAN LOOK IT OVER DURING LUNCH.
I'M SHORT, SO I'LL HAVE TO BE THE SETTER. IS THAT OKAY?
Humph...
IT'S NOT THAT I LOVE STUDYING.
Thanks.
You're welcome.
INUKAI!
THINK YOU CAN HELP ME MAKE A POSTER LATER?
YOU WERE THE ASSISTANT INSTRUCTOR IN YOUR MIDDLE SCHOOL CALLIGRAPHY CLASS, WEREN'T YOU?
SURE!
I'd be glad to help.

IF YOU GIVE YOUR ALL TO A TASK...
...POSITIVE RESULTS WILL FOLLOW.
...
Boy...
I'm impressed...
...that you're able to take on so much.
INUKAI, YOU SURE ARE MULTITALENTED.
1-1
YOU THINK SO?
IT DOESN'T MATTER WHETHER IT'S SCHOOLWORK, SPORTS OR YOUR SOCIAL LIFE, YOU EXCEL AT THEM ALL. IF I HAD A DAUGHTER AND YOU WERE HER BOYFRIEND, I'D HAVE NOTHING TO WORRY ABOUT.
I'd love having you as a son-in-law.
WHAT ARE YOU TALKING ABOUT?
OKAY, ALL JOKES ASIDE. YOU DON'T HAVE A SINGLE WEAKNESS, DO YOU?
I'VE NEVER SEEN YOU FLUSTERED.
You always look calm and collected.
I bet nothing stresses you out.
...

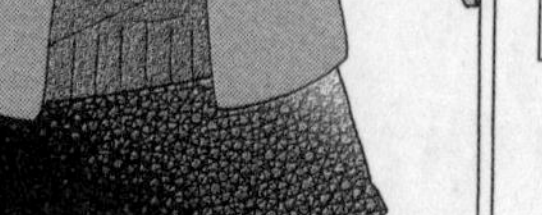

COME TO THINK OF IT...
I'VE NEVER...
...REALLY GIVEN IT MUCH THOUGHT.
I'm not afraid of bugs or ghost stories, for that matter.
RATTLE

KOFF
TSURU!!
YOU'RE FINALLY BACK?!
YES!! I WAS SICK WITH A COLD FOR A WHOLE WEEK!
ARE YOU SERIOUS? THAT SUCKS!
I was won-dering who that masked delin-quent was...
OH, SHUSH!
CHUCKLE CHUCKLE
THAT'S RIGHT. THERE WAS A STUDENT WHO'D BEEN OUT SICK SINCE ENROLLING AT THIS SCHOOL.
SO THAT'S KAME'S FRIEND ...
I THINK HER NAME WAS...

THAT'S MONICA TSURUTANI. SHE'S A QUARTER EUROPEAN.
HA HA HA HA
She is?!
HMM...
WHIP
I THINK SHE HAS SOME SPANISH IN HER...
OH?
YOU'VE ALREADY TALKED TO HER?
NO. KAME FILLED ME IN.
OH YEAH?
SPAIN...
BARCELONA...
GAUDI...
WHAT ARE YOU WRITING, INUKAI?
HUH...?
OH!!
This week's Paella

I MADE A MISTAKE.
CORRECTED →
This week's goal: Zero Tardies
I'M HOME...
TMP TMP TMP
BIG BRO!
BRAID MY HAIR! ♪
MOM COULDN'T BRAID IT FOR YOU?
YOU'RE WAY BETTER THAN MOMMY.
HMM... ALL RIGHT. HAVE A SEAT.
YES, SIR! ♪
OH WELL...
A BRAID...

IT'D BE EASY TO DO WITH HER HAIR...
GASP!
BIG BRO!
MY HAIR'S ALL MESSY!
OH, I'M SORRY!!
MESSY
STRANGE...
HAVE I BEEN A LITTLE DIS-TRACTED LATELY?
UMPH
SAY...

ARE THOSE THE MATH NOTE-BOOKS?
ARE THEY DUE TODAY?
UH...
UH-HUH.
THUUUD...
?!
OH GOODNESS... ARE YOU ALL RIGHT?
SORRY. I DIDN'T MEAN TO STARTLE YOU. I'LL PICK THEM UP.
WHY AM I MAKING SO MANY MISTAKES?
HERE...

I DON'T HAVE ANYTHING TO DO, SO I'LL CARRY HALF.
YOU'RE ALWAYS SO BUSY, INUKAI.
YOU DESERVE A BREAK EVERY ONCE IN A WHILE.
GIGGLE
WHAT?
UH, THANKS.
I APPRECIATE THE HELP.
THAT MIGHT...

"YOU DESERVE A BREAK EVERY ONCE IN A WHILE."
...HAVE BEEN THE FIRST TIME...
...ANYONE'S GIVEN ME A HAND.
IT'S NO USE!!
I CAN'T FOCUS!!
WHAT'S WRONG WITH ME?
...
...
...

THUD
RICH
MILK
Rich in Calcium.
WHAT ARE YOU DOING DRINKING MILK, MANABU?
GULP
GULP
GULP
JOLT
OH, WELL...
...
168 cm →
Maybe I'll have some too.
OHHH...
?
RAAAH
Run!
Run!
Go!

KOSH
WHZZ
YES! GOOOAL!!
WAY TO GO, INUKAI!!
I'll give you a kiss later!!
No, thank you!
GOOD LUCK!!
GOOD JOB, BOYS!
THAT'S THE FORMER CAPTAIN OF THE MIDDLE SCHOOL SOCCER TEAM FOR YOU...
I JUST GOT LUCKY.

Oh, the boys are playing soccer.
INUKAI, HEADS UP!!
OH!
HUH?
MISSED
OHHHHH!!
DON'T WORRY ABOUT IT!
IT'S RARE FOR INUKAI TO MISS LIKE THAT!

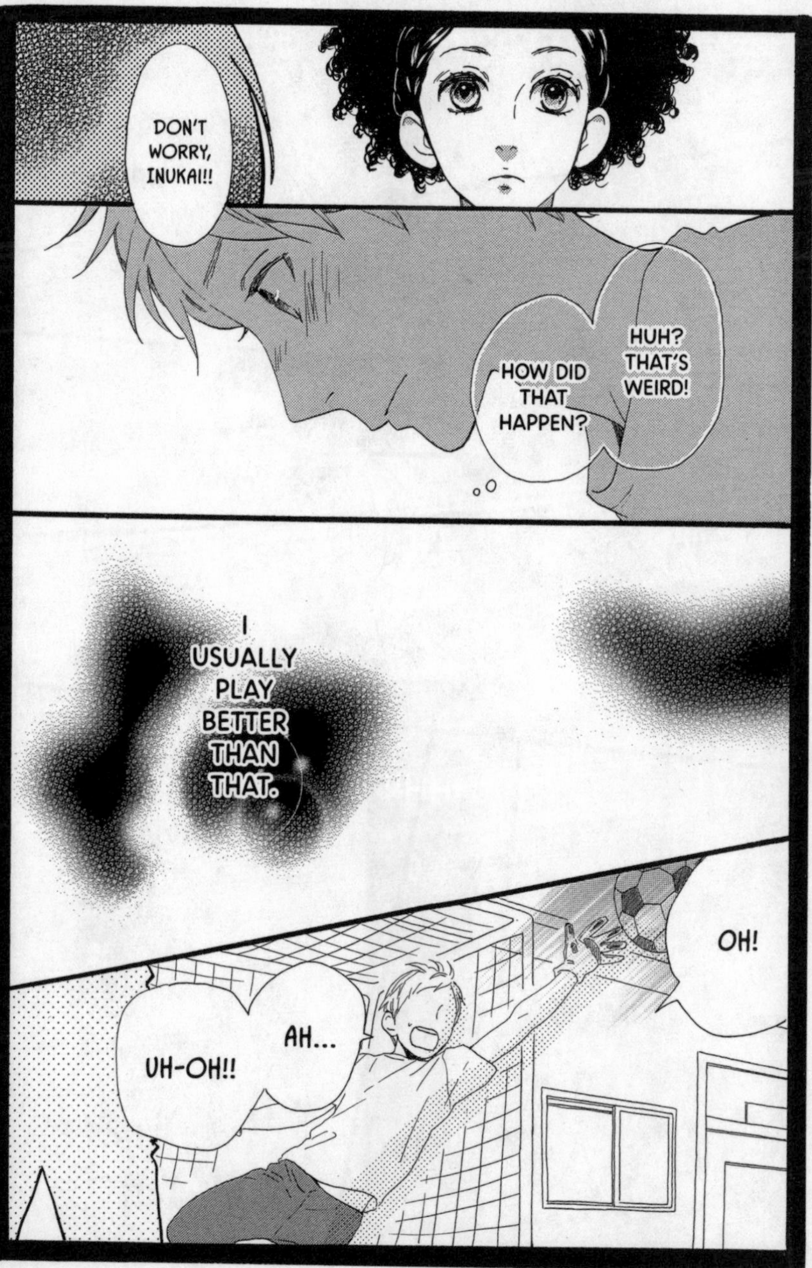
DON'T WORRY, INUKAI!!
HUH? THAT'S WEIRD!
HOW DID THAT HAPPEN?
I USUALLY PLAY BETTER THAN THAT.
OH!
AH...
UH-OH!!

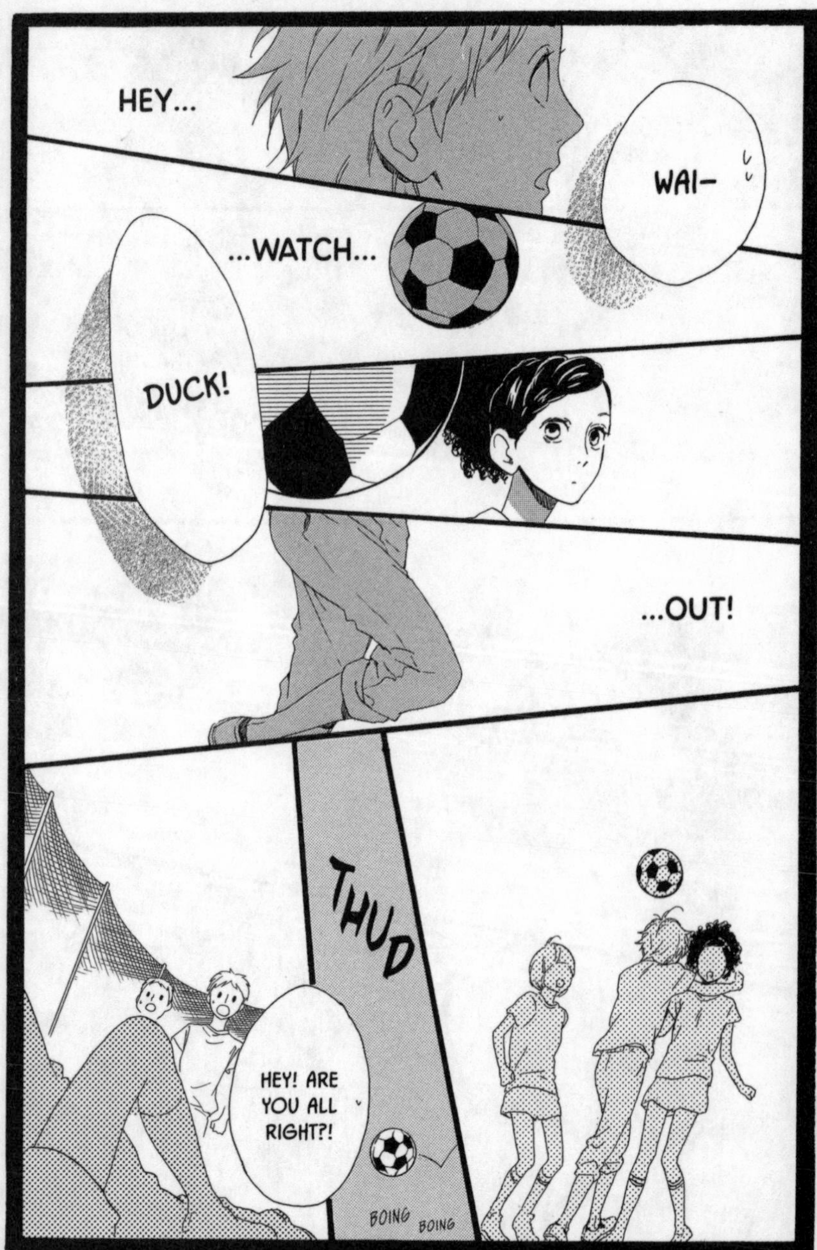
HEY...
WAI-
...WATCH...
DUCK!
...OUT!
THUD
HEY! ARE YOU ALL RIGHT?!
BOING
BOING

I THINK SO...
HUH?
THUD
THUD
What's
this?
...
A...
ARE YOU ALL RIGHT?

I'M SO SORRY!! I...
OH, FORGET IT.
I'M FINE. NO NEED TO WORRY!!
SEE? THANK GOODNESS I'M NOT INJURED!!
WHIP
PLOP
OH...
HUH?
DRIIIP
OH... WHAT SHOULD I DO?

WHEN I'M NEAR TSURU...

...THINGS GO HORRIBLY WRONG.

IT'S AS IF MY TRUE COLORS ARE BEING REVEALED.

YOU'RE UP?!
OH!
THEY SAID YOU SHOULDN'T GET UP YET.
LIE BACK DOWN.
I'LL GET YOU A COLD TOWEL.
W- WHAT SHOULD I DO?
THUMP
THUMP
THUMP
I HAVE TO APOLOGIZE.
ZAA...
BUT...BUT WHAT SHOULD I SAY?
UH... I'M TERRIBLY SORRY FOR WHAT HAP- PENED? NO, THAT'S TOO FORMAL!
Maybe the comedic approach.
...FOR EARLIER...
THANKS...

YOU KNOW...
HUH...?
WHEN PEOPLE SEE THE WAY I LOOK, THEY DON'T EXACTLY JUMP AT THE CHANCE TO HELP ME OUT.
I WAS TOUCHED BY WHAT YOU DID.
I...
I DIDN'T...
...PROTECT YOU AT ALL...
I JUST KEPT EMBARRASSING MYSELF.
EVEN THOUGH YOU'RE A GUY, I DON'T FIND YOU ANNOYING.
YOU KNOW...
OH... NEVER MIND ABOUT THAT.
SHOCKED

WELL, THIS IS A SURPRISE.
YOU'RE GOOD AT EVERYTHING, AREN'T YOU, INUKAI?
NO WONDER THEY CALL YOU MR. PERFECT.
IT'S ONLY NATURAL THAT EVERYONE WOULD DEPEND ON YOU.
WELL, I'LL BE GOING BACK TO CLASS NOW.
I left the towel near your bed.
TUK
HUH?
HER HANDKERCHIEF...?
Oh!
Are you all right...
...Inukai?!

IT'S A CUTE DESIGN.
TSURUTANI ACTED LIKE...
...SHE WASN'T FAZED BY WHAT HAPPENED, BUT...
...ACTUALLY, I THINK IT REALLY BOTHERED HER.
OTHERWISE, WHY WAS HER HEART BEATING SO FAST?
SHE IS...

...A LOT NICER...
...THAN SHE LOOKS.
MORE SO THAN ANY WOMAN I'VE EVER MET.
I AM NOT MR. PERFECT.
2-2 Potato
FES
LET'S SEE...
INUKAI, YOUR HEIGHT...
170
165
160
...IS 169 CM.

WHAT?!
NOW YOU CAN WEAR A MEDIUM.
169 CM?!
Really?!
YES.
Next, I'll measure your waist.
YAY!! I'VE GROWN!!
WHAT'S UP? I'VE NEVER SEEN YOU THIS EXCITED.
DID SOMETHING GOOD HAPPEN?
HUH?
WELL... LET'S JUST SAY I'VE MADE SIGNIFICANT STRIDES IN ONE OF MY WEAK AREAS.
HUH?
WHAT'S THAT MEAN?
I'M MANABU INUKAI.

MY FAVORITE SUBJECTS ARE HISTORY AND MATH.

MY FAVORITE SPORT IS SOCCER.

IN MIDDLE SCHOOL, I WAS BOTH STUDENT BODY PRESIDENT AND SOCCER TEAM CAPTAIN.

THE AREA I'M WEAKEST IN IS...

IT'S MY ACHILLES' HEEL!

YOU ARE MY ONLY WEAKNESS.

SINCE I FIRST SAW YOU...

...I'VE DONE NOTHING BUT MAKE A FOOL OF MYSELF IN YOUR PRESENCE.

BUT SOMEDAY...

...I'LL MUSTER UP THE COURAGE TO TELL YOU HOW I FEEL.

WHEN THAT DAY COMES, I HOPE YOU'LL LISTEN...

...AS I POUR MY HEART OUT.

<The End>

About "Inukai's Story."

I believe I wrote this during the year-end observances last year....!! It didn't take long to write at all.... The love between Inukai and Tsuru has been quietly progressing in the backdrop of the main story. Their love story is so peaceful.

Inukai's face is very easy to draw, but for some reason, I couldn't nail him down in the rough draft. Why is that? Probably because, sadly, he and I have nothing in common. But his father is one of my favorite characters.

Afterword

So...what did you think? Huh? My afterword is too short? I'm sorry. I plan to add more scribbles in the next volume.
Oh, the next volume will include a crossover with *Hibi Chocho*. I'm hoping that I'll have the opportunity to draw various things. (Like when I worked on the lettered pages with Suu Morishita.)
Hopefully, by then, our HP will have been replenished...

It doesn't look like him.
He is hard to draw, Suu Morishita.
He has an oval-like face.

See you again

in the next volume.

Special Thanx:

Editor U

My assistants:

Kame-chan, Noborio, Nils Machimura

Designer Kawatani

The people at the print shop

Members of the editorial staff at *Margaret*

And all of my readers!

See you soon!

I hope you won't give up on this story, despite Shishio gradually leaning toward the dark side.

—Mika Yamamori

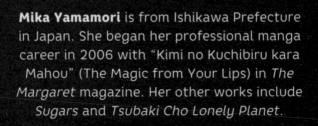

Mika Yamamori is from Ishikawa Prefecture in Japan. She began her professional manga career in 2006 with "Kimi no Kuchibiru kara Mahou" (The Magic from Your Lips) in *The Margaret* magazine. Her other works include *Sugars* and *Tsubaki Cho Lonely Planet*.

★DAYTIME★SHOOTING★STAR★ 10

SHOJO BEAT EDITION

Story & Art by
Mika Yamamori

Translation ★ **JN Productions**
Touch-Up Art & Lettering ★ **Inori Fukuda Trant**
Design ★ **Alice Lewis**
Editor ★ **Karla Clark**

Printed in the U.S.A.

Published by VIZ Media, LLC
P.O. Box 77010
San Francisco, CA 94107

10 9 8 7 6 5 4 3 2 1
First printing, January 2021

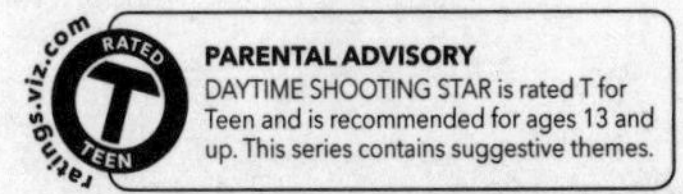

Romances by IO SAKISAKA

STROBE EDGE

When Ninako meets Ren, the handsome, enigmatic guy that all the girls worship, her life takes an unexpected turn. With just a few words and a smile, he changes her world...

Ao Haru Ride

As soon as Futaba realized she really liked Kou in junior high, he had already moved away. Now, in high school, Kou has reappeared, but is he still the same boy she fell in love with?

Love Me, Love Me Not

Fast friends Yuna and Akari are complete opposites—Yuna is an idealist, while Akari is a realist. When lady-killer Rio and the oblivious Kazuomi join their ranks, love and friendship become quite complicated!

VIZ

STOP!

You may be reading the wrong way!

In keeping with the original Japanese comic format, this book reads from right to left—so action, sound effects and word balloons are completely reversed to preserve the orientation of the original artwork.

Check out the diagram shown here to get the hang of things, and then turn to the other side of the book to get started!

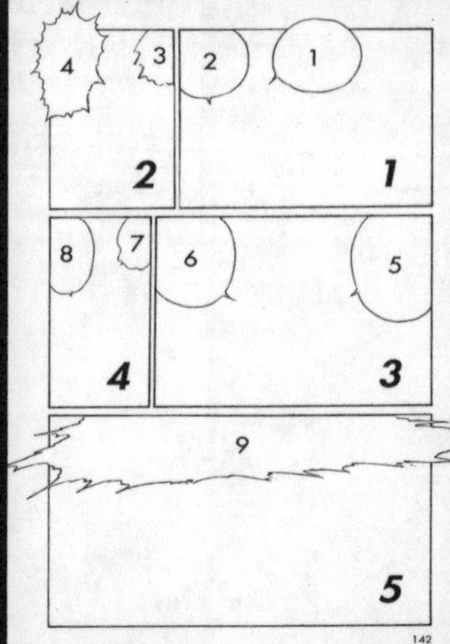